Worldwide optimal state system

for a maximum of fair distribution, self-determination & quality of life

Bibliografische Information der Deutschen Nationalbibliothek:
Die Deutsche Nationalbibliothek verzeichnet diese Publikation in der Deutschen
Nationalbibliografie; detaillierte bibliografische Daten sind im Internet über http://dnb.dnb.de
abrufbar.

Herstellung und Verlag: BoD – Books on Demand, Norderstedt

ISBN: 978-3-7481-5774-8

Content

In one sentence

The basic features of a worldwide optimal state system can be described relatively simple in one sentence:

In the interests of the well-being and wealth of all humans, each human creates a future-oriented & positive-solution-oriented, peaceful, emotionally distant, sovereign fundamental will, recognizes every human's inherently valid, inalienable right to an equal share of space and resources, evolution-based knowledge & a fair share of publicly offered goods, strives with regard to life-sustaining & -improving processes (such as renewable energy- & resource production cycles, assignment of transaction-simplifying value symbols, possibility-creation of a tension field overlay-free population density) for simple, worldwide, and as far as possible independently feasible, expandable solutions for long-term conflict & problem-solving and awards all humans the right to act freely at will, as long as the common good is not endangered and the rights and freedoms of other humans are not restricted.

In order to better understand the individual points, they are described in more detail separately and their idea and meaning are examined.

Basic attitude

Every human creates a future-oriented and positive-solution-oriented, peaceful, emotionally distant, sovereign will in the sense of the well-being and wealth of all humans.

An optimal system can not be determined by a preponderance of congruities, but is constructed by logic and reason.

A state system created by democracy, that is to say, a system created by a majority of votes, automatically becomes an anarchy for all voters if no completely fair, global state system is chosen (which is why you do not have to vote because there is only one option anyway), because no clear-thinking human will settle without a fight with an unfair system, which would result in choosing another option.

In order to permanently avoid war, unrest and disputes over space, resources and law, only a - in the will of the prosperity of all humans - fair-distributing system will work, which is built on truth and solvability and does not seek reasons to exclude other humans to allow individuals or a group to have a more comfortable life in the short term.

A demarcation of the territory and / or an exclusion of humans is a predatory concept based on repression that creates a warlike scenario rather than a colossal empire.

The concept of repression permanently leads to self-destruction, as it tends to misjudge the need to solve critical problems.

Humans have enough natural enemy images such as overpopulation, illnesses & deficiencies, so they do not have to fight needlessly to satisfy competitive emotions. In addition, humans live enlightened enough to be able to talk openly about sexual desires, and in the negative case are able to do without them, since modern humans are self-confident enough to cope with rejection because they have many other ways to satisfy their emotions. In addition, sport provides a controlled opportunity to reduce competitive emotions while maintaining a community-friendly attitude.

These points indicate that a functioning state system must be applicable worldwide.

For the successful, efficient execution of life-saving acts, an emotionally distanced basic will creates the best opportunities to provide a broad mental overview, including factors relevant to the future, whose change can improve the overall situation in the long term - sovereignty creates a scenario of the uninterruptibility of one's own thoughts, which leads to conduct an uninterrupted examination without external influences.

Defining the ego by not having to define oneself and thus not providing an attack surface by a non-existent value-creation creates a low-vibration, emotionally distant atmosphere ideal for investigation purposes, while unwanted / annoying negative or positive residual emotions are removed through awareness of their irrelevance to the solution progress.

The state of sovereignty is established by the concentration of thought-streams in the brain area when the heart chakra is tense. The peaceableness arises automatically by combining these factors due to the consciousness of being superior to potential attackers.

Problems can only be solved in the present and in the future; therefore, it is important to grasp the core problem without being seized by short-term emotions that may have been the cause of poor problem solving.

Humans strive for simple, global solutions that can be implemented and extended by other humans as independently as possible to support life-sustaining and improving processes for long-term conflict and problem-solving.

Problems are solved in the basis of their true origins; a symptom-fighting for short-term emotional gratification is waived.

Deep-seated competitive thinking is a perversion in the face of a booming global economy, as it develops blocking symptoms, which is represented by e.g. occupational groups or excessive control thinking, which in the long term are not only useless, but also counterproductive, because the problem origins are not examined and corrected in the base.

Most crimes happen due to a lack of space, resources and / or rights and are to be understood as symptoms of a misconceived state system; a fair distribution of space, resources and rights instead leads to the prevention / reduction of such acts.

Many professions are nonsensical in their attempt to protect humans from acts and trying to find "scapegoats" for a not functioning system, rather than realizing that these acts are the logical consequence of a faulty system; among other things, some professional groups (for example, the legal profession, collection agency, police, judiciary, security service) try to make money by acting against humans who legitimately take whatever they are entitled to because of a lack of resources - creating willfully an inequality in the process.

Nonsensical control and surveillance not only lead to reduced quality of life for all humans, they are also completely useless, since they don't correct the real misery´s origins or deliberately disregard them - either from evil will, which could refer to a lack of sexual openness and/or self-determination or a fear of confrontation caused by a knowledgeable lack of positive solutions. It also leads to the obstruction of the work flow, which perverts the entire world system; instead of producing abundant and high-quality products, which would result in abundance for every human and needlessness of control, because generosity could prevail, workflow, freedom and quality of life will be reduced by harassment with the result that the entire system suffers unnecessarily and only then actions emerge out of scarcity against which countermeasures were taken because of wrong fears and / or greed.

In a generous, mind-oriented state system, with regard to restrictions, sales personnel and money are unnecessary, since they primarily have a controlling and braking character.

Those who have value symbols at their disposal usually have no reason not to pay (or deliberately don't to highlight existing deficiencies), and those who have none have the right to a life-sustaining share or sufficient material due to properly distributed space and resources anyway.

In the case of scarcity, humans act generously in the life assurance and fair sharing sense.

To get accurate results for all forms of partitions involving a large amount of variables, e.g. the world's surface, space, and the number of living humans, a lot of tedious and often frustrating work is required, most of which is completed too late and thus unusable; however, since the world and its humans always involve constantly changing dynamics, a precise division is neither necessary nor desirable, since in the sense of wealth and therefore necessary buffer zones to avoid possible bottlenecks, it is mandatory to calculate generously in the sense of the inclusion of every human anyway.

Rights

Every human recognizes every human's inalienable, valid from birth right to

- an equal share of space and resources, both in terms of size and mass as well as usability

- a fair share of publicly offered goods worldwide

- a fair share of value symbols (money) that symbolizes the fair share of publicly offered goods worldwide

Even without available money, there is always a right to publicly offered, life-sustaining goods if, due to the current situation, the claimable share of space and / or resources can not be accessed and / or the technological means / knowledge of a human is not sufficient to produce the necessary goods.

- evolution-based knowledge

As far as knowledge-providing institutions (schools, academies, universities) are concerned:

Grades as an indirect praise or punishment are wrong for several reasons:

On the one hand, they motivate humans to allow themselves to be influenced by the evaluations of other humans, instead of evaluating their work / performance soberly according to their own goals and values; by doing so, they not only weaken their own ability to judge by neglecting training and become indirectly dependent on irrelevant sources, but also gain the impression that praise or censure is decisive for their ability to perform, which can lead to corruption and manipulability.

The achievement is already the reward; body and mind are trained and energized, a life-enhancing good or scenario is created and in the economy it increases the variety of options and thus contributes to the common good.

In addition, rankings motivate humans to see themselves as adversaries rather than co-operation partners, and for later life purposes are completely irrelevant numbers that are unrelated to a human's capabilities, since benefits are will, environment, and daytime forms, and the teaching qualities are perceived differently from human to human and actually are, as different sympathies develop and consequently different communication patterns.

Due to human auras and thought pattern overlays unequal team achievements are created, which make a rating of a single human completely useless.

Languages are dynamic and a matter of interpretation anyway; if humans want to understand each other, they do so wordlessly; if they do not want to understand each other, no language helps.

It is much more important, through authentic self-living, to teach humans from the beginning that securing life and solving the problems associated with it, as well as fair, generous thinking in the context of community affairs, are essential for a successful life. In this framework, problems should be discussed and solved, and critically dealt with a potentially flawed world.

In this respect, school is - up to elementary training - a kind of occupational therapy, which can produce a proper interaction when it is correctly interpretated by students and teachers, as long as there is no opportunity for self-employment and / or a matching sexual partner was not found.

Compulsory education does not exist anyway.

- Free acting at will, as long as it does not limit the freedom of other humans and the common good is not endangered

Any form of arbitrary hierarchy is an indirect declaration of war on humans; no clear-thinking human wants to submit to a creature of his own kind.
Every human is the supreme controlling body of himself, maintaining as many rights and freedoms as possible without endangering his or her balance with the rights and freedoms of others.

These rights are often claimed only symbolically in full due to the human life dynamics and in the sense of economy and manageability.

Fair allocation of space, resources & goods

The proportion of space is made up of the four areas of flora and fauna, transfer and community space, agricultural area and personal living space.

Flora & Fauna, transfer & community space and agricultural land are often used in cooperation with other humans to preserve nature, to maintain and improve the transfer routes, for recreational opportunities and for efficient goods production and processing, while personal living space is used mostly private for habitat design, personal preferences and self-actualization of the owner.

The area proportion (R) is calculated by dividing the total area (G) by the number of living humans (M), in short $G / M = R$.

An area surface (B) is calculated by dividing the area proportion (R) into four parts, in short $R / 4 = B$, or dividing the total area (G) by the number of living humans by four, in short $(G / M) / 4 = B$.

The resource share (Ra) per resource is calculated by dividing the respective resource mass (Rm) of a quality class by the number of living humans (M), in other words $Rm / M = Ra$.

Humans provide life-sustaining & improving goods and knowledge about their production globally even, before advancing technological, to enable everyone's living standards to be improved similar.

Resources are often processed into goods under collaboration after pooling resource shares (Ra).

When processing resources, care is taken to ensure that, if possible, a reproducible extraction process is maintained or produced.

Fair symbolic share of publicly offered goods worldwide (value symbols (money))

In order to maximally simplify goods transactions and property transfers, humans manufacture valid value symbols (money) worldwide.

This share amount (A) allocated to each human monthly at the beginning of the month in the form of value symbols (money) is calculated from the dividing of the estimated sum of the prices of all material, intellectual and service goods (S +) offered for the first time in the previous month by the number of living humans (M), in short S + / M = A.

The prices of the goods correspond to their estimated values in terms of life assurance and quality of life maintenance & improvement.

The value of abstinence:

In an efficient system, work processes can often be handled by a small number of humans producing products that meet the consumption needs of a relatively large number of humans. It is important to recognize that the humans not actively participating in the cooperation to ensure an efficient production cycle may be part of the working group and in this case have to be rewarded fairly, because they are not hindering the process by their abstinence (in contrast to blindly searching for inadequate integration), and the space and resources are entitled to them through fair division and natural law.

It is important that the colaborating workers acknowledge this fact and are not mistaken in their belief, that the humans holding themselves back are not entitled to their fair share.

Large parts of the bureaucracy are superfluous, because the right to a fair share of worldwide publicly offered goods lasts lifelong for every human and thus concepts such as pensions and insurance, debts, interest and all financial transactions, which unnecessarily affect the flow of life and create imbalances, are unnecessary, because there are abundant resources available to every human and there is the possibility to switch to self-sufficiency through the claimable space and resource share.

This ensures both that each human receives enough money every month to secure their standard of living, and that the humans who produce a lot have the advantage of being able to make more money if they strive for it, since the products remain in their possession until sale.

Thus, the optimal balancing act between life support and life improvement, between solidarity and competition has succeeded. Peaceful humans do not have to worry about being marginalized, and competitive humans have the opportunity to reward their productivity.

The fair symbolic share of worldwide publicly offered goods is paid to humans of all ages and regardless of their wealth and income; to young humans as a symbol to recognize them as full members of society from the beginning, and secondly, to satisfy the the expansionary urge that will arise in the course of their development; to wealthy humans as a sign of inclusion and to not punish them for their increased work urge.

Possible award text for value symbols:

Worldwide currency handed to any human for positive result-oriented work, the decline of negative destructive work or as a fair symbolic share of publicly offered goods.

Only valueable under the assumption, that any human is entitled to obtain a fair share of publicly offered goods worldwide by nature´s right and by logic of a peace-serving distribution.

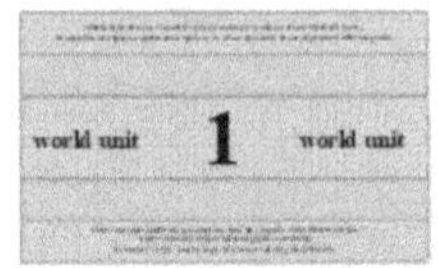

world unit 1 world unit

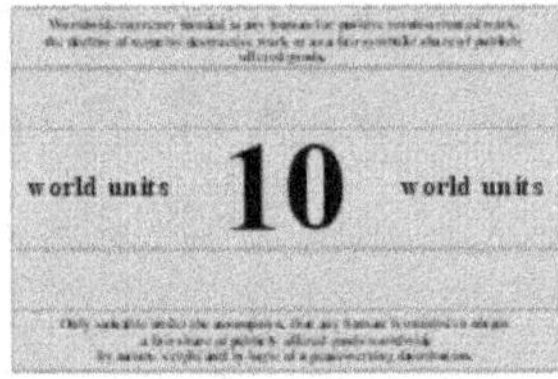

Worldwide currency handed to any human for positive result-oriented work, the decline of negative destructive work or as a fair symbolic share of publicly offered goods.
world units 10 world units
Only valuable under the assumption, that any human is entitled to obtain a fair share of publicly offered goods worldwide by nature's right and by logic of a peace-serving distribution.

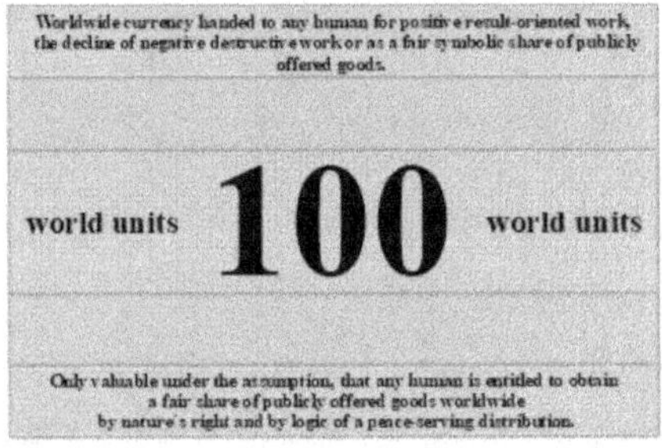

Worldwide currency handed to any human for positive result-oriented work, the decline of negative destructive work or as a fair symbolic share of publicly offered goods.
world units 100 world units
Only valuable under the assumption, that any human is entitled to obtain a fair share of publicly offered goods worldwide by nature's right and by logic of a peace-serving distribution.

Worldwide currency handed to any human for positive result-oriented work, the decline of negative destructive work or as a fair symbolic share of publicly offered goods.
world units 1000 world units
Only valuable under the assumption, that any human is entitled to obtain a fair share of publicly offered goods worldwide by nature's right and by logic of a peace-serving distribution.

Population density

Children are created out of the altruistic will of life-giving, when their producer's life is fulfilled and - apart from the normal everyday dynamics and desired disputes - running smoothly; an ulterior motive, to impose upon them a world, to educate them, or to get an advantage through their existence, can lead to unnecessary complications that can negatively affect overall world dynamics. Spatial foresight on the part of producers leads humans to grow up in the best possible accessible environment in which they live self-determined and learn the vital processes.

Humans take care of the production of the possibility of a tension field overlay-free population density.

An overpopulated world is a breeding ground for suffering and misery; smothering diseases, disease transmission & will restrictions lead to listlessness and physical and mental decline and as a result contribute to a negative climate - mutual restrictions lead to power struggles, rapes, strife, wars and could be avoided by prospective floor plans in terms of easy extensibility / restructuring in view of upcoming / planned births or the change of location for life assurance / -optimization.

In case of overpopulation, humans do not produce children and the best possible distribution is sought.

In the case of borderline situations, humans do not produce more than 1 child per capita - one begotten child can be credited with half a head per producer;
thus, in the case of separation, there is no dispute as to who the child is to be attributed.

It is a matter of course - first a functioning system must be constructed before it is extended; children should be able to grow up in an environment that offers all the benefits that their growers can access.

Advantages

• Bureaucracy and control can be reduced to a minimum and gain only indicative, book-keeping character, because due to a thriving global economy and a generous attitude richness for every human can be produced and thus scarcity and loss fears are resolved

• due to similar living conditions, barrier-free communication is possible

• Humans work primarily to maintain their own body and mind, resulting in a healthy biorhythm, resulting in a high quality of life and long life

• Humans can use good quality products because there is no shortage due to performance pressure

• wealthy humans are not afraid of assaults, because everyone is in a solid starting position

• long legal paragraphs / records become unnecessary, since situational analyzes can be derived from the basic set of legal understanding through the use of one's own understanding

 • Pension becomes superfluous, as rights to space, resources and goods are life-long - eliminating unnecessary bureaucracy

• Work resulting from humans not being able to solve their own problems is diminishing and space for new world-enhancing work and / or leisure is created

• there is no need to perform placeholder work in order to have an alibi call, as humans realize that not doing nonsensical, destructive work is also a valuable work because it requires discipline and mental strength

• by recognizing that freedom, living space, self-determination, and health are paramount, there are fewer sick humans on the planet

Definitions / Word dictionary

alibi - proof of evidence

analysis - investigation

anarchy - lawlessness

atmosphere - environment

barrier - obstacle

democracy - popular rule

distanced - by far available

dynamic - changing state

emotion - feeling

complication - difficulty

conflict - mutual lack of direction

communication - message exchange

optimal - best possible

option - possibility

process - multi-unit operation

quality - value

wealth - a state of freedom that demands no action in the sense of safeguarding
one's life in the medium to long term, because a significant excess of vital resources
is available in the case of a natural course of the future, thus leaving maximum
freedom for shaping the present and the future
relevant - important
rhythm - repetitive sequence
situation - interaction of several facts
sovereign - situation superior
symbol - factual summary sign
system - cooperative structure of several items
currency - character to describe the state